The King of Kings

Treasures of the Vatican Library
(Book Illustration)

The King of Kings

Turner Publishing, Inc.

ATLANTA

The illustrations in this book are taken from Latin volumes in the collections of the
Vatican Library, including the Barberini, Capponi, Chigi, Borghese, Ottoboni, and
Rossiano collections. The sources for each illustration appear on page 80.

Published by Turner Publishing, Inc.
A Subsidiary of Turner Broadcasting System, Inc.
1050 Techwood Drive, N.W.
Atlanta, Georgia 30318

First Edition 10 9 8 7 6 5 4 3 2 1
ISBN: 1-57036-103-7

Printed in the U.S.A.

Treasures of the Vatican Library:
Book Illustration

*T*HE KING OF KINGS, a small volume in the Treasures of the Vatican Library series, offers a selection of miniature masterworks of book illustration from the collections of one of the world's greatest repositories of classical, medieval, and Renaissance culture. The Vatican Library, for six hundred years celebrated as a center of learning and a monument to the art of the book, is, nevertheless, little known to the general public, for admission to the library traditionally has been restricted to qualified scholars. Since very few outside the scholarly community have ever been privileged to examine the magnificent hand-lettered and illuminated manuscript books in the library's collections, the artwork selected for the series volumes is all the more poignant, fascinating, and appealing.

Of course, the popes had always maintained a library, but in the fifteenth century, Pope Nicholas V decided to build an edifice of unrivaled magnificence to house the papacy's growing collections—to serve the entire "court of Rome," the clerics and scholars associated with the papal palace. Pope Sixtus IV added to what Nicholas had begun, providing the library with a suite of beautifully frescoed rooms and furnishing it with heavy wooden benches, to which the precious works were actually chained. But, most significantly, like the popes who succeeded him, Sixtus added books. By 1455 the library held 1,200 volumes, and a catalogue compiled in 1481 listed 3,500, making it by far the largest collection of books in the Western world.

And the Vatican Library has kept growing: through purchase, commission, donation, and military conquest. Nor did the popes restrict themselves to ecclesiastical subjects. Bibles, theological texts, and commentaries on canon law are here in abundance, to be sure, but so are the Latin and Greek classics that placed the Vatican Library at the very heart of all Renaissance learning. Over the centuries, the library has acquired some of world's most significant collections of literary works, including the Palatine Library of Heidelberg, the Cerulli collection of Persian and Ethiopian manuscripts, the great Renaissance libraries of the Duke of Urbino and of Queen Christiana of Sweden, and the matchless seventeenth-century collections of the Barberini, the Ottoboni, and Chigi. Today the library contains over one million printed books—including eight thousand published during the first fifty years of the printing press—in addition to 150,000 manuscripts and some 100,000 prints. Assiduously collected and carefully preserved over the course of almost six hundred years, these unique works of art and knowledge, ranging from the secular to the profane, are featured in this ongoing series, Treasures of the Vatican Library, for the delectation of lovers of great books and breathtaking works of art.

And she gave birth to her firstborn son and wrapped him in bands of cloth, and laid him in a manger, because there was no place for them in the inn.

LUKE 2:7

In that region there were shepherds living in the fields, keeping watch over their flock by night. Then an angel of the Lord stood before them, and the glory of the Lord shone around them. . . . But the angel said to them, "Do not be afraid; for see—I am bringing you good news of great joy for all the people: to you is born this day in the city of David a Savior, who is the Messiah, the Lord."

LUKE 2:8–11

When they had heard the king,
they set out; and there, ahead of
them, went the star that they had
seen at its rising, until it stopped
over the place where the child was.
When they saw that the star
had stopped, they were
overwhelmed with joy.

MATTHEW 2:9–10

On entering the house,
they saw the child with
Mary his mother; and they
knelt down and paid him homage.
Then, opening their treasure chests,
they offered him gifts of
gold, frankincense, and myrrh.

MATTHEW 2:11

Now after they had left, an angel
of the Lord appeared to Joseph
in a dream and said, "Get up,
take the child and his mother,
and flee to Egypt, and remain
there until I tell you; for Herod
is about to search for the child,
to destroy him."

MATTHEW 2:13

. . . when Jesus had been baptized, just as he came up from the water, suddenly the heavens were opened to him and he saw the Spirit of God descending like a dove and alighting on him. And a voice from heaven said, "This is my Son, the Beloved, with whom I am well pleased."

MATTHEW 3:16–17

Jesus said to him,

"Receive your sight;

your faith has saved you."

"But so that you may know
that the Son of Man has authority
on earth to forgive sins"—he said to
the one who was paralyzed—
"I say to you, stand up and take
your bed and go to your home."

Then suddenly a woman who had been suffering from hemorrhages for twelve years came up behind him and touched the fringe of his cloak. . . . Jesus turned, and seeing her he said, "Take heart, daughter; your faith has made you well." And instantly the woman was made well.

MATTHEW 9:20, 22

Then people came out to see
what had happened, and when
they came to Jesus, they found
the man from whom the demons
had gone sitting at the feet of Jesus,
clothed and in his right mind.
And they were afraid.

LUKE 8:35

When he had said this,
he cried with a loud voice,
"Lazarus, come out!"
The dead man came out,
his hands and feet bound
with strips of cloth, and
his face wrapped in a cloth.
Jesus said to them,
"Unbind him, and let him go."

JOHN 11:43-44

And Jesus said to him,

"Foxes have holes, and birds

of the air have nests; but the

Son of Man has nowhere

to lay his head."

MATTHEW 8:20

For as the lightning
comes from the east
and flashes as far as
the west, so will be
the coming of
the Son of Man.

MATTHEW 24:27

"Do not judge, and
you will not be judged;
do not condemn, and you
will not be condemned. Forgive,
and you will be forgiven. . . ."

LUKE 6:37

Jesus said to them,
". . . Walk while you have
the light, so that the darkness
may not overtake you.
If you walk in the darkness,
you do not know where
you are going."

JOHN 12:35

MNIPOTENS

"Come, follow me," Jesus said,

"and I will make you fishers of men."

MATTHEW 4:19

"... For truly I tell you,
if you have faith the size of a
mustard seed, you will say to this
mountain, 'Move from here to there,'
and it will move; and nothing
will be impossible for you."

MATTHEW 17:20

While they were eating, Jesus took a loaf of bread, and after blessing it he broke it, gave it to the disciples, and said, "Take, eat; this is my body."

MATTHEW 26:26

Then he took a cup, and after giving

thanks he gave it to them, saying,

"Drink from it, all of you . . ."

MATTHEW 26:27

". . . for this is my blood of the covenant, which is poured out for many for the forgiveness of sins."

"I tell you, I will never again drink of this fruit of the vine until that day when I drink it new with you in my Father's kingdom."

MATTHEW 26:29

He came a third time and said to them, "Are you still sleeping and taking your rest? Enough! The hour has come; the Son of Man is betrayed into the hands of sinners."

MARK 14:41

Then Jesus said to him,
"Put your sword back into
its place; for all who take the
sword will perish by the sword."

Pilate said to them, "Then what should I do with Jesus who is called the Messiah?" All of them said, "Let him be crucified!"

. . . So when Pilate saw that he could do nothing, but rather that a riot was beginning, he took some water and washed his hands before the crowd, saying, "I am innocent of this man's blood; see to it yourselves."

MATTHEW 27:22, 24

. . . and after twisting some thorns
into a crown, they put it on his head.
They put a reed in his right hand and
knelt before him and mocked him,
saying, "Hail, King of the Jews!"
They spat on him, and took the reed
and struck him on the head.

MATTHEW 27:29-30

Those who passed by derided him, shaking their heads and saying, "You who would destroy the temple and build it in three days, save yourself! If you are the Son of God, come down from the cross."

MATTHEW 27:39–40

And about three o'clock Jesus

cried with a loud voice,

"Eli, Eli, lema sabachthani?"

that is, "My God, my God,

why have you forsaken me?"

MATTHEW 27:46

Then Jesus, crying with a loud voice, said, "Father, into your hands I commend my spirit." Having said this, he breathed his last.

LUKE 23:46

Now when the centurion
and those with him, who were
keeping watch over Jesus, saw the
earthquake and what took place,
they were terrified and said,
"Truly this man was God's Son!"

MATTHEW 27:54

Then Joseph bought a linen cloth,

and taking down the body,

wrapped it in the linen cloth,

and laid it in a tomb that had

been hewn out of the rock.

He then rolled a stone against

the door of the tomb.

MARK 15:46

And suddenly there was
a great earthquake; for an angel
of the Lord, descending from
heaven, came and rolled back
the stone and sat on it.

MATTHEW 28:2

His appearance was like lightning,

and his clothing white as snow.

For fear of him the guards shook

and became like dead men.

MATTHEW 28:3–4

Jesus said to her,
"Do not hold on to me,
because I have not yet ascended
to the Father. But go to my
brothers and say to them,
'I am ascending to my Father
and your Father, to my
God and your God.'"

JOHN 20:17

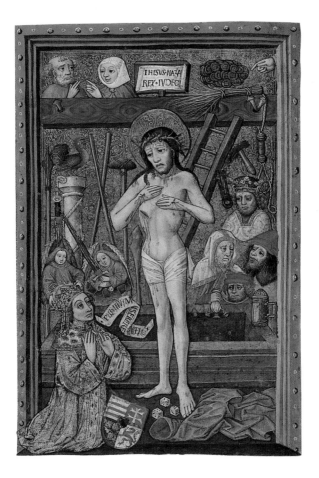

"Look at my hands and my feet;

see that it is I myself.

Touch me and see; for a ghost

does not have flesh and bones

as you see that I have."

LUKE 24:39

And Jesus came and said to them, "All authority in heaven and on earth has been given to me. Go therefore and make disciples of all nations, baptizing them in the name of the Father and of the Son and of the Holy Spirit . . ."

So then the Lord Jesus,

after he had spoken to them,

was taken up into heaven

and sat down at the

right hand of God.

MARK 16:19

Cover, half-title page, and frontispiece: Latin volume 3769 in the Vatican Library Collection; p. 7: Latin volume 3769 in the Vatican Library Collection; p. 8: Latin volume 183 in the Borghese Collection; p. 11: Latin volume 3781 in the Vatican Library Collection; p. 12: Latin volume C VII 205 in the Chigi Collection; p. 15: Latin volume 3770 in the Vatican Library Collection; p. 16: Latin volume 3781 in the Vatican Library Collection; p. 19: Siriac volume 559 in the Vatican Library Collection; p. 20: Siriac volume 559 in the Vatican Library Collection; p. 23: Siriac volume 559 in the Vatican Library Collection; p. 24: Siriac volume 559 in the Vatican Library Collection; p. 27: Siriac volume 559 in the Vatican Library Collection; p. 28: Latin volume 381 in the Barberini Collection; p. 31: Latin volume 94 in the Rossiano Collection; p. 32: Latin volume 613 in the Barberini Collection; p. 35: Latin volume 610 in the Barberini Collection; p.36: Latin volume 112 in the Urbino Collection; p. 39: Latin volume 112 in the Urbino Collection; p. 40: Latin volume 119 in the Rossiano Collection; p. 42: Latin volume 3805 in the Vatican Library Collection; p. 45: Siriac volume 559 in the Vatican Library Collection; p. 46: Latin volume 610 in the Barberini Collection; p. 49: Latin volume C VII 205 in the Chigi Collection; p. 50: Latin volume 218 in the Capponi Collection; p. 53: Latin volume 3769 in the Vatican Library Collection; p. 54: Latin volume 381 in the Barberini Collection; p. 57: Latin volume 3769 in the Vatican Library Collection; p. 58: Latin volume 3769 in the Vatican Library Collection; p. 61: Latin volume 3769 in the Vatican Library Collection; p. 62: Latin volume 614 in the Barberini Collection; p. 65: Latin volume 3781 in the Vatican Library Collection; p. 66: Latin volume 3770 in the Vatican Library Collection; p. 69: Latin volume 381 in the Barberini Collection; p. 70: Latin volume 3805 in the Vatican Library Collection; p. 73: Latin volume 1164 in the Rossiano Collection; p. 74: Latin volume 112 in the Urbino Collection; p. 77: Siriac volume 559 in the Vatican Library Collection; p. 78: Latin volume 585 in the Barberini Collection. Ornamental illumination on pp. 9, 13, 14, 17, 18, 21, 22, 25, 26, 29, 30, 33, 34, 37, 38, 41, 43, 44, 47, 48, 51, 52, 56, 59, 60, 63, 64, 67, 68, 71, 72, 75, 76, and 79 is from Latin volume 8700 in the Vatican Library Collection.